SUCCESS

A Handbook for Developing the Right Mindset and Achieving Your Dreams

By: Fred Mercado

Table of Contents

Introduction

I want to thank you and congratulate you for downloading *Success: A Handbook for Developing the Right Mindset and Achieving Your Dreams*!

Everyone seems to have their own definition of success, yet there is still a unanimous judgement when someone does not live up to the vision of conventional success. The general universal image of success typically covers the bases of economic or financial status, marital status, level of education, and career prestige. The concept of success in all of these areas of life is that if you can tangibly or visibly show progression and development relative to another person's standards, then you are successful. The pressure to be successful in the eyes of other's can cause severe stress and even existential crisis. In today's society, we consciously live with the thought that somewhere someone is judging and comparing us. This mental state, along with many other factors, has attributed to many people giving up on achieving their unique idea of success and living out their personal dreams.

Giving up on your dreams and losing your focus in achieving your goals can lead you to become stagnant, in every aspect of your life. The constant fear of failing or being looked down upon by others inhibits us from taking risks and doing what is necessary to achieve our goals and be happy. When we come to a standstill, our mental state and personal happiness suffers. Humans are meant to hunt, to search and go after what they want even if it involves taking chances. When we do not progress in accordance to our individual objectives, we lose our vision.

This book contains proven steps and strategies on how to become a truly successful individual according to your own standards, dreams, and goals. You might have already researched this topic a lot, or maybe not at all. You might be thinking that this is just another bogus generic book that is going to give you unspecific information that fits into the "one-size fits all" category. But I assure you, this is not that kind of book. This book contains invaluable tips and steps that you can take to truly get you back on track, motivate you to adapt a positive mental attitude, and teach you how to take control of your life.

This book is meant to be used as a daily reference guide for anyone who feels like they have lost their vision and ambitions in life as a result of the chaotic and competitive world that we live in. The purpose of reading this handbook is to assist you in refocusing on getting your mind to see situations and challenges as opportunities to succeed. By itemizing the primary issues that keep people from accomplishing their dreams and ambitions, this book will guide you through re-training your mind to develop the proper mindset needed for achieving success.

Here's an inescapable fact: millions of people are unaware that the cause of their anxiety, depression, unhappiness, and regret is the subconscious feeling that they have failed at life in some way. This book is not just for self- employed driven business men, or the middle- aged accountant who feels like she is missing something in her life. This book is for anyone and everyone who genuinely feels like they need or want to steer their life in a positive direction, in a way that will further their journey towards achieving their dreams. No one wants to feel like they have failed. No one goes through life believing that missing out on opportunities and not growing as an individual is the most authentic form of living or achieving success. That is why reading and understanding the information in this book is so important.

If you do not develop your mindset into a positive and uplifting state, then you will not feel fulfilled or satisfied with any part of your life. This may sound scary or intimidating, but the reality is that if you do not wake up and become self- aware of the path that you are traveling, then you will become filled with regret, resentment, and anger. The good news is that it is never too late to take control of your life and become successful in your own eyes. And it does not matter what success truly means to you. Whether you view success as losing ten pounds or getting a promotion at work or getting married and starting a family; this book will help you break down your mental limitations and live the life of your dreams.

Regardless of whether you are an entrepreneur or a stay at home parent, you have most likely already come up against a situation that has challenged and weakened your willpower and mental state. Everyone faces this challenge at multiple points in their lives, it is completely normal. But locating your inner motivation to persevere and work past your previous and future physical and mental obstacles is what makes you stronger. The real challenge is not letting yourself default into the mindset that your confidence, ideas, or abilities is not enough to overcome these setbacks. While some people believe that overcoming obstacles means gritting your teeth and powering through them is what leads to success and stronger willpower, such a tactic does not work for everyone. Simply dealing with daily stressors does not make you more confident or help you get closer to your goals. Coping with your problems will only weigh you down and fatigue you, making you more vulnerable to give in to any negative thoughts that come from future problems.

One of the goals of this book is to overcome your physical and mental burdens by using positive methods that propel you further to become stable and successful. Success can only be built on a solid foundation, through positive reinforcement and affirmations, identifying causation, refocusing your mindset, setting appropriate goals, and fueling your motivation and willpower. All of these steps will be thoroughly discussed in the upcoming chapters of this book. Soon you will learn that true fulfillment and happiness can only be attained by redefining what constitutes success in your own mind.

Congratulations on taking your first step towards finding your true purpose and becoming your most authentic self. While reading about how to become successful is easy, taking action and understanding how to make that positive change is the most difficult challenge you will face. You are already on your way to becoming your best self. Just keep working towards bettering yourself, and the results will speak for themselves. Enjoy the journey and learn as much as you can. Good luck!

"Rock bottom became the foundation on which I rebuilt my life." -J.K. Rowling

Chapter 1: What Causes Loss of Ambition?

Remember when you were a child, and people used to ask you, "what do you want to be when you grow up?" Your answer may have been incredibly ambitious, like a professional dancer, an astronaut, or a wizard. Or maybe you knew that being a fireman or nurse was your true calling. Regardless of what your childhood fantasized career was, you did not doubt yourself or your intentions. You believed that you truly could become the first person to make a bubble gum that tasted like roast beef and a baked potato, or travel around the world in a hot air balloon. The games that you played and the toys you had only fueled your dreams and ambitions. Even if your parents were extremely strict and made you practice the violin everyday against your will, their love and support made you feel like all of your hard work could lead to a seat in the Philharmonic Orchestra.

The amount that others believed in you truly did make you trust that there were endless possibilities and open doors. You were told that the sky was the limit, so you could achieve anything you put your mind to no matter what. But as you and millions of others ventured throughout the world, everyone lost that mindset. We were told "no" by a certain person or a number of people, and suddenly all of that hope and self- assurance was washed away. What you failed to realize at that point was that their opinion was the one that mattered the least. What you did not realize was when the prospective employer said you did not get the job, it was not the worst result to have ever come from putting yourself out there. The truly worst result was you believing that that person's final say was a truth; a reflection on who you are as a worker, parent, spouse, or as a human being.

But what was the real cause of your loss of ambition? You may know that recent moment of epiphany, when you realized you were unhappy or stuck. But what was the cause of your downward spiral or stagnant state? In this chapter, we are going to explore what causes people to lose their ambition and drive. For many people, there is not just one inciting incident. In most cases, the epiphany comes from a long development of being unfaithful to their authentic selves. It is a combination of all the times you agreed to something you did not want to do, when you lied about how you truly feel, and giving up on an opportunity because you were too afraid of failing or it not working out.

There are a number of factors that have led you to purchase a book on achieving success in correlation with altering your mindset. The fact of the matter is that the mind is a powerful tool. Not only does your brain control the rest of your body and how you function, but if you can make yourself truly believe something, your mind will bring it into fruition. For example, if you see someone who is sick and tell yourself that a virus is going around and that you definitely are experiencing symptoms, then your body will reflect those thoughts. Suddenly a random sneeze is a sign of the flu and you are being diagnosed at the doctor's office. The point is, your mind controls the reality around you. So if you believe that you truly can achieve success and be happy, it will happen. The only person that you need to convince is yourself.

Losing your ambition is correlated with four different factors: motivation, enthusiasm, age, and milestones. While you can probably name a dozen more specific causes of your ambition loss, most cases can be traced back into one of these four categories. The most encouraging idea is that your mindset is what determines how you react to discouraging circumstances generated by one of the following elements.

Motivation

The definition of motivation is a reason/ reasons for acting or behaving in a certain way. Motivation is what gets you up in the morning. It is what makes you go to work and spend eight hours reading emails on the computer. Your motivation in life can be any number of things or people: your family, friends, pet, wanting to make a lot of money, wanting to be happy. You go to work because you are motivated to feed yourself by earning money. You go to your child's little league game because you want to see him succeed. Even the smallest reasons behind your motivation make a huge impact in how you live your life every single day.

What motivates you?

Is it wanting to be the best at your job? Is it a fear that your spouse will stop loving you? Can you identify any sources of motivation in your life? Can you not come up with a single one? The answers to these questions to not really matter, but they do put into perspective the importance of why you do things; *what* drives you to do the things you do every day. Motivation is the reason that you have everything in your life today. It is why you are in a relationship, employed, wealthy, healthy. Motivation is a powerful tool that drives you to attain and achieve anything you want in life, regardless of any barriers in front of you. With enough motivation, you can accomplish any goal or dream.

However, motivation is also the culprit behind your loss of ambition. It is why you feel depressed, unsuccessful, resentful, and lost. Motivation is a tool, and should be used actively and frequently. It is a skill that wears down when you do not practice it enough. As you suspend your motivation, all other areas in your life begin to stagnate. You stop making progress and start to lose whatever developments that you made. Motivation is the reason you stopped working hard or caring. It is why you lost yourself while trying to deal with life and all of its chaos. You lost your motivation, and now you have lost your ambition.

Your amount of motivation in life determines the seriousness and importance of your goals, as well as your success. When you lose your motivation in life, you start to lose progress and the purpose of why you started working hard in the first place. Your vision for your life is driven by the amount of motivation you have. Without ambition, you have no motivation. And without motivation, you have no ambition. Both strengthen one another, but one trait can be lost at the expense of the other.

Have you ever wanted to learn another language or get a certificate in personal training? You have a sudden and brilliant realization to get up and do something, to take action and create driven by an urge so strong that you feel unstoppable. But after a few days or even a few hours, you lose steam and evidently give up on your goal brought on by a spontaneous burst of passion. Do not worry, you are not alone in this. Very frequently, people become motivated to do or accomplish something. But this type of motivation is often short lived and fades after a while.

Why do you experience this sudden rush of motivation, only to have it evaporate after a little while? One of the reasons is that you do not really want to achieve the thing that inspired you. You are too busy with everything else going on in your life that you forget about it. Changing your routine or daily habits it too hard and would require too much effort for you to actually dedicate time towards something that could drastically change your life. To accomplish your goals, it takes a constant effort and motivation to keep yourself working towards it. Motivation can be easily sparked, but not so easily maintained.

Do you know the feeling you get after reading a really inspirational quote? Or after hearing a song that just speaks directly to your soul? That is motivation. The goal is to keep that feeling alive and burning until you have fulfilled the objective you were inspired to tackle. There are dozens of reasons that lead you to lose that initial motivation and desire to do something different. You need to find your motivation for keeping your ambition alive. Without motivation, you have no reason to continue doing anything you typically accomplish on a daily basis or new challenges that can better your life.

People normally lose their motivation to complete any task when they believe that they have failed or are not good enough to continue trying to achieve their dreams. But motivation is the ultimate mental exercise. Motivation is like a muscle; it must constantly be put to use. And the more you use it, the stronger your motivation becomes. But the less you practice motivation, the more you lose.

Enthusiasm

Even if you have a ton of motivation to accomplish your goals, if you lack enthusiasm and passion, then you have no reason to keep working on your motivation or ambitions. Enthusiasm is having profound enjoyment, interest, or passion for something. While motivation is the reason for you to continue working towards your goal every day, enthusiasm is the passion and interest that keeps that goal and your motivation alive. Why would you continue working towards something that no longer makes you happy or excited?

Many people go through their lives doing things that do not actually matter to them. They go to work at a job they do not love or even have a relative interest in simply because it pays their bills and puts food on the table. They have the motivation, but the loss of enthusiasm has resulted in a loss of ambition. Passion is what drives us to take on new challenges, new relationships, and other opportunities. Without passion, your life becomes dull and repetitive; you begin to do things out of habit, rather than interest. You no longer cook for your spouse because you genuinely want to do something nice, but because you have been doing it for the past fifteen years. Lack of enthusiasm is the silent killer of relationships, career goals, and health and fitness dreams.

The real question is what drove you to lose your passion? What happened to the enthusiastic young individual who was excited to go to job interviews and blind dates? Do you believe that you settled for less than what you wanted or deserved? Or maybe you believed that you truly deserved less than what you dream of? One of our biggest problems is that we limit ourselves to what we are given, even if it is less than what we wanted because we are afraid of not coming across anything better. Our enthusiasm is weighed down by our low expectations, because we believe that if we were good enough to get something better, we would have gotten is already. We put ourselves into the mindset that because we found a place we are comfortable in, we should not search for something else because it may never come along.

A great example of this, that is relatable to millions of people around the world, is your job. We are told that as soon as we finish school, we need to find a job that we plan on staying at for at least a few years. Sure, we might move over to another company *once*, but for the most part people stay where they are. Because they are comfortable, safe, and believe they are an asset to that company because of the years of work and experience they have put into it. But suddenly your college dream of becoming a CEO of a large company turns into contentment of at least being a part of that company. As your enthusiasm dies down, so does your ambition. Then suddenly, thirty years have passed and you realized that you had given up on your career goals.

You should never give up on your passion, regardless of what anyone says or how many times you fail. Even doing one small thing a day to keep your passion alive, it is worth putting in that little effort to eventually see your dreams flourish. Kiss your spouse, look for a job in your dream career, buy some new cooking equipment. If you lack passion, your motivation and ambition will be powered by habitual conditioning, rather than genuine interest or excitement.

Age: It Isn't Just a Number

We are told that "age is just a number" throughout our lives. We use it as an excuse to date someone older or go on a crazy adventure that isn't typical for our age group. But the philosophy of using age as an excuse to do things is never applied when it comes to relocating your ambition. Here is a perfect example of what I am talking about: a fresh- faced college graduate takes a chance on a job opportunity, despite having very little experience and being up against slightly older competitors. He is encouraged by friends and family to go to the job interview anyway because regardless of his age, he still is qualified to be considered. However, if a middle-aged man with years of experience at the same company thinks about leaving, his entire future and lifestyle is in jeopardy. He is told that he is too old to go up against recent graduates and should stay where he is out of fear for his financial safety.

Age creates mental barriers that keep us from going after our dreams and embracing new experiences. Telling someone that they are too old or too young to do something perpetuates that mindset throughout society. That person is going to relay the same perspective to their friends, family, and children. Age creates two forms of fear: the fear of missing out on your chance, and the fear that your opportunity is long gone. Here is an example of the fear of missing out on your chance: parents tell their children that they only get two sets of teeth: their baby teeth and their adult teeth. While trying to instill proper dental hygiene habits, parents will still tell their children that getting a cavity is okay because that tooth will be gone soon anyway. This idea inspires children to eat as much sugar and candy as they can, because in a few years that opportunity will be gone forever.

Of course this example is a bit sad and puts blame on the parents; so here is another example. In the United States, a person's twenty- first birthday is a huge deal. You gather a group of friends and spend the whole night drinking and making the excuse that because it is your birthday, you can do any crazy thing you want to. But what if some elements of that ideal birthday do not allow you to have that typical experience? What if you don't have a large group of friends who want to go out with you? What if you get injured or sick and can't go out to the bar? What if you do go out and end up having a terrible time? Suddenly your typical twenty- first birthday is a lost experience that you cannot get back.

The same idea is applied to the fear that you have already missed your opportunity. This is usually the mindset of older folks who believe that their younger years were the best they have ever had. Your years of work and life experience have given you invaluable wisdom and skills, yet you are afraid to take chances that might jeopardize everything you have earned in life. If you take a chance on a startup company and leave your day job, then your home and family is put at risk. Even if you do not own a house or have children, people will warn you that your lifestyle may be too valuable to give up because of some spontaneous surge of motivation.

Age makes us limit ourselves, making us believe that because we are too young or to old, we are not able to have certain life experiences. While the obvious exceptions to this are real, such as dating someone who is a minor while you are well past the age of eighteen, there are plenty of opportunities that are still open to you, even if is seem unconventional for someone of your age. Here are some mental barriers that you can break right now: you are not too old for a yoga class or working out, you can learn a new language, you can travel the world, you can go out to the bar to find a date.

You do not have to limit yourself just because society has set standards for you. You do not have to give up on your dreams and goals because you are too old or do not have enough experience yet. Age is just a number; a number that can either motivate you enough to ignite your ambition, or make you live with the regret that you missed out on priceless opportunities.

Milestones

How do you measure a year? Usually with milestones: occasions that call for celebration, mark a beginning or end to something, or times of distress or achievement. Typically, milestones are birthdays, holidays, graduations, sending your child off to college, having an operation, or a birth or death in the family. All of these constitute as measurements of our year: how much progress we have made or events that mark an important time in your life. The problem with measuring your progress with milestones is that it sets you up for failure.

Milestones may initially spark enthusiasm and motivation, but can cause stress and fear when you are faced with possible failure. If you are inspired to use a milestone to mark the beginning of new habits, but then fail to live up to your own expectations, then you see yourself as a failure. And if you use milestones as a measurement for when you need to accomplish a task, but fail to complete it by that time, then you have failed again.

The most popular milestone across the globe is New Year's Eve. New Year's resolutions do wonders for gyms that are selling discounted memberships. New Year's Eve offers people an excuse to try and adopt new habits while dropping the old, unhealthy ones. If you want to quit smoking or lose

9

weight, the last hurrah on New Year's Eve is the perfect farewell party to kick your old ways to the curb. You work hard for about a few weeks, busting your butt at the gym and chewing nicotine gum. But what happens a few months afterwards? You begin to lose motivation and the initial spark of inspiration has died down into cravings and the pressure of old and familiar habits. New Year's Eve now seems pretty far away, and there is always next year to try and change your ways. Now you are back to smoking half a pack a day and eating takeout every other night.

Using milestones to mark the beginning of a new goal provides you with the perfect excuse to quit once that milestone is out of sight. Did you know that more than sixty percent of people who have gym memberships do not actually go to the gym? Thousands of people sign up for new memberships in January, but stop going by the time March rolls around. That is because the enthusiasm of New Year's has died and being healthy does not seem as important as it was a few months before.

Using milestones to mark the end of your journey is just as self- destructive. Many people, especially students, love to put off project and goals until the last second. And in the end, they can usually produce some product that is just a shadow of something that could have been greater, if there was more time and effort put into it. When you set a goal for yourself to achieve six months down the road, you will have the initial motivation that gets you to take action at first. But in a few weeks you convince yourself that six months is more than enough time to get work done, so you can relax for now. Suddenly, five months has gone by and you have made no progress and may be even farther away from your goal than before. Now you have the perfect excuse to put off your goal or give up altogether.

What happens if you do not meet your goal in time? Chances are, it is going to make you feel terrible and incapable. Your enthusiasm for your dream is gone, and your ambition was lost in the middle of your journey. Milestones allow excuses to enter the equation, which is something that you cannot afford. If you want to be successful and find your ambition again, then do not give yourself a chance to make excuses. Whether it is the fear of your age or the mindset that you missed your chance and should wait for the right time. The right time is *now*. You do not need some grand sign or spiritual awakening to start working on yourself and being successful. The only thing stopping you, is the mental barriers in your own mind.

Chapter 2: Where Did You Lose It?

Did you ever have that small epiphany, where you are in the middle of doing something that you have done for the past X amount of years, and realize that you are not where you want to be in life? Maybe it was when you were in the middle of typing an email at the office, and thought "why am I still at this job? I want to be (fill in the blank.)" Or perhaps it was when you were taking your kids to school and realize that you never did get around to take that tour of Europe you dreamed about in college. Lack of success does not necessarily mean regret, but it will if you do not reassess why you do not feel successful or ambitious in all aspects of your life. There is nothing wrong with being content at your job or loving the carpool conversations with your children. For many people, it is the small things that make their day worth all the stress and chaos.

However, you should still always be working towards fulfilling a goal; whether it is a lifelong dream or a short-term project. Your ambition does not suddenly disappear, it slowly fades away as you compromise your dreams and goals for instant gratification. When it does come time to make a decision and face a challenge that will allow you to get one step closer to achieving success, you convince yourself that you do not have enough resources to competently address the challenge. Whether it is money, confidence, intelligence, or time; you once again put off making progress because in some way, you feel like you are not ready or able.

Every small step or challenge we face in the process of achieving our goals, is viewed as a huge leap of faith into the abyss. We all have days when we just do not want to do anything; and after working all week and stressing out about bills, who can blame us for wanting one day off? Especially when we are suffering from an illness, discouragement, or just lethargy. For many people who have lost their motivation, they experience overwhelming feelings of failure and lack of ambition in correlation with their current situation. An example of this is getting your spouse to work your shift at the little league concession stand and pinning the problem on not wanting to do it. But the real issue is that you feel like you are going to do a bad job and fail, just like with other challenges you have faced.

These feelings are often subconscious to us, but they continuously affect us every single day. Everything you do on a daily basis: the small decisions you make, how you react in response to problems or stress, and your mental attitude are all symptoms of your fear of failure and lack of ambition. But this symptom applies to almost everyone. The same excuses are used time and time again, without even realizing the damage it is doing to your mental state. Completely able bodied people spend their days essentially doing nothing more than sitting on the coach or walking around like a zombie. This behavior lasts for weeks, months, and even years on end. Many people believe that this kind of habitual living cannot be stopped unless some great force or epiphany wakes them up. An event like a heart attack, a diabetes diagnosis, losing a loved one, or filing for bankruptcy does not happen to everyone. So you should not wait around for something big to happen to make a change in your life and snap out of the robotic behavior that keeps you from achieving your goals.

What has kept you from going after your dreams? What decisions have you made that have kept allowing you to put off your goals? Was it giving up on scheduling business meetings to help your spouse shuttle your children back and forth between their playdates? Was it convincing yourself that one slice of cake would not ruin your diet completely whenever you had the chance to eat dessert? It is hard to imagine the effect these decisions can have on your success and life at the time you make them. But even just a few months down the line, those choices contribute to your feelings of discouragement and failure. They keep you from further pursuing your goals by giving you enough of an excuse to put it off one more time. This behavior takes a toll on your career and relationships.

Motivation and enthusiasm are driving forces that inspire you to continue pursuing your vision of success. But when you lose your ambition, your motivation and enthusiasm suffer and lead you to compromise your happiness and success for less than what you want and deserve. One of the hardest challenges of working towards your dreams is finding enough inner strength to spring into action. When you lose your ambition, it is usually because you lost your confidence, refuse to accept responsibility, or do not realize that your old dreams are not what you truly want anymore. In this chapter, we are going to explore where you first lost your ambition; whether it was when you compromised your beliefs to make someone else happy or believed that your failure was another person's fault. You know the reasons behind your lack of ambition and how it deters you from achieving success. Now you must learn how locating the specific point in time where you began to doubt yourself is the next step towards overcoming mental barriers that keep you from accomplishing your goals.

While reading this chapter in particular, keep in mind that I do not know your life story. I do not know your personal struggles or specific reasons why you gave up on your dreams. But from experience and research, I know that mostly everyone's current mental state can be traced back to specific moments when their confidence and attitude were tested and damaged. But regardless of what your moment in time was, being able to identify why it steered you down a different path will help you get back on your feet and ready to achieve the success you have always wanted.

Confidence and Self- Esteem

In middle school or high school, you probably learned about the value and impact of self- esteem in your health class. At the time, self- esteem seemed like a joke, that having low self- esteem meant you were sad or weak. But as you grew older, and developed physically and mentally, your self-esteem wavered and you began to doubt yourself. Suddenly you were not as smart as you thought you were, or as good looking, or artistic, or athletic. Other people challenged your abilities and mental state until your confidence was at an all-time low. It does not matter when you had this experience, but that you recognize that it happened and it hurt you. Maybe it was when John handed in a kick- ass report that made yours look like an amateur put it together. Or when you were twenty minutes late to pick up your child and the head of the PTA greeted you with an attitude.

It does not really matter whether or not this experience was *the* defining moment that make you decide to stop pursuing your dreams. Because it still made an impact. It affected you and made you doubt yourself when you were more than capable. Try to think back to one of those moments. How did it make you feel? Did you change yourself because of it? When we do not fall into that perfect mold of confidence and capability, we change how we are. Not that changing ourselves is necessarily a bad thing (it is not), but we begin to alter who were are to please other people. If one particular person makes us feel inadequate, we might try to mimic yourselves to be more like their image. But that is not staying true to yourself. Altering the way others see you to try and gain confidence or another person's approval not only inhibits you from being successful, but pushes you farther away from your goals.

The only positive and appropriate justification for changing yourself is with the intention of self- development. Self-development is putting is time and effort in order to become the best version of yourself. Self- development allows you to work on yourself, in all possible aspects, in order to be the best person you can be. While working on yourself, your confidence is naturally boosted and you feel like you are making real progress. Confidence is knowing that you can accomplish your goals and be successful, regardless of what anyone says or how many times you fail at something. Doesn't that sound a lot better than trying to mimic someone else's behavior in order to make others think that you believe in yourself?

Real confidence does not come from playing games, with others or yourself. You cannot trick yourself into having high self- esteem. And why would you want to when you can have the real thing with just a little time and effort? People lose confidence in themselves when they believe that who they are or what they have to offer is not good enough. Being turned down for a job does not mean you are stupid; it means that you should learn even more about the field so you can be more knowledge about it. Every time someone tells you "no" or your confidence waivers, remember that every "negative" experience is another opportunity to learn and grow.

The problem lies with the fact that when people lose their confidence, their ambition also goes out the window. They refuse to take action and work towards progress. Inaction leads to failure, laziness, and discontent. Once your ambition and confidence are gone, you begin setting the bar too low for yourself; giving up your goals because you do not believe you can reach them.

Don't miss out on opportunities to make your dreams come true. When you believe in yourself, you are allowing yourself to reach your peak potential. Confidence is teachable, it is not something that some humans are born with and others are not. Some people believe in the phrase "fake it until you make it." But that philosophy does not apply to your major goals and aspirations, and is definitely not a long- term sustainable mindset. You *can* teach yourself to build your confidence and become successful by believing in yourself; which we will talk about in the upcoming chapters.

Take Responsibility and Hold Accountability

Let's just make one thing clear right away... no one is responsible for your lack of ambition or lack of success except for you. I know this sounds harsh, but the mindset of blaming other people for your problems is not going to bring you good fortune or make you feel any better about where you are in life. Sure, you can try to blame your crappy childhood on why you cannot hold stable long- term relationships, or your siblings throwing you into the pool for your fear of water. Although we associate negative memories or events on our present behavior and habits, those occurrences do not *have* to affect your life. You do not have to blame your past on your current problems or future actions. Why? Because it really all comes down to your mental state.

But let's go back to the beginning before diving in to how taking responsibility can change your life and make you successful. Too often, we like to pass the blame and use other people as scapegoats to avoid facing our problems. This usually comes from a fear of being associated with failure and being punished. Take for instance a time when you were a child and blamed your siblings on something you did that you knew was going to get you in trouble. If your parents found out you were the culprit, then you would have to face their disappointment and a punishment. As you grew older and became an adult, you still use this tactic for dealing with your problems. You blame forgetting to pick up your wife's dry cleaning on the dry cleaner's closing early. Or pretend that you were not the last one to finish the pot of coffee and blame Jerry for taking the last cup and not refilling it.

17

But not only does passing the blame mean convincing others that you are free of liability, it also means convincing yourself. This is where the most damage to your mental state comes from; telling yourself that the failure is not your fault and that someone else is more accountable to your lack of success than you are. Your kids had a soccer game, so you did not have time to read Tony Robbin's book on starting your own business. Dalton at the office is much smarter than you when it comes to marketing, so you should probably take the backseat on the new business project. You can keep telling yourself these small lies to keep the spotlight off of the chance of you failing; or, you can take action and do something great to gain the recognition you want and deserve.

When we pass off responsibility, we allow ourselves to fade into the background of our own lives and allow them to deteriorate. Each time you pass the blame, you are letting go of your goals, dreams, and chance at success. You should not give up your fitness goal of going down two pants sizes just because you father was overweight. You do not have to fulfill anyone's expectations of failure because it seems right, natural, or impossible to overcome. The sad part is that almost everyone has been conditioned to pass the blame onto something disassociated with ourselves for the parts of our life we are unhappy with. We blame our spouse, parents, boss, friends, the economy, the government, the weather— any outside source that is not directly linked to our actions. But the real problem is you.

Success can only be achieved when you take one hundred percent responsibility for your life. You are not poor because you were born into an impoverished family. You are not overweight because your mom has weight issues. You need to give up on all of your excuses and self-victimizing attitude; everything that has kept you from taking action and going after what you want.

When a situation occurs in which you become discontented, afraid, or embarrassed, ask yourself: "how did my actions create this?", "What did a say or not say that caused this to happen?", "How did my behavior get the other person to react that way?", "What can I do differently next time to achieve the result I wanted?"

You cannot change the weather, the seasons, or the circumstances around you: but you can take personal responsibility and change yourself. One of the greatest myths of today is that we are entitled to a great life. Now, more than ever before in history, we believe that someone else, somehow, is responsible for our happiness, financial status, health and wellness, and career opportunities just because we exist. But there is only one person who is responsible for the quality of your life: and that person is you. You create your present conditions. Therefore, you can dismantle them and re-create them until you have the life you desire. You are responsible for everything in your life that happens or doesn't happen to you.

Losing Yourself

In the beginning of the first chapter, we talked about your goals and aspirations as a child. We talked about how the motivation you felt when you were younger fueled your dreams of success and steered you towards opportunities that would help bring you closer to attaining your goals. But then you started making decisions that made you give up your ultimate dreams for instant results, despite the fact that your choices would not bring you any closer to what you truly wanted. Many college professors argue that the person you were as a child and as a young adult was a result of your upbringing. You adopted your parents' beliefs and habits and missed the chance of forming your own thoughts and opinions. While this theory can be applied to certain habitual conditions, it is not necessarily true.

As we grow older and are more exposed to a variety of opinions, views, and beliefs, we doubt our own. Sure, learning another person's point of view is important for our own development, tolerance, and awareness; but staying true to yourself is much more important. In today's world, everyone is so consumed with voicing their opinion and having it count, that we are losing our own identities. Now, if someone finds out you have an opposing viewpoint, they will spend hours trying to convince you that they are right and you are wrong. You are called ignorant, a bigot, close-minded, and a number of immature names but because you did not hop on the bandwagon and agree with the person scolding you. This happens online with social media, over text messages, in person, and even news outlets have resorted to this kind of behavior. But this is just one instance that makes us doubt our own beliefs and compromise our values to meet the demands of society.

The example above is a bit generic and may not have been experienced by everyone, so let's dive a little bit deeper into the real issue. Your dreams are a genuine reflection of who you are as a person – your values, beliefs, morals, fears. If your dream is to be a millionaire, it reflects the value you give money, a possible fear of being poor or in need, that you put stake into material objects, or are very ambitious. If your goal is to be a humanitarian, it reflects your morals of helping others in need, giving back to the world, being a good person, or wanting to be a caregiver.

The reason why you are reading this book is because you lost your motivation and are doubting your dreams or current place in life. There are a number of reasons that you do not identify with your current circumstance or your goals. One reason is that the life you have now does not add up to the vision that you have in your head. You wanted more for yourself, but compromised somewhere in the past and ended up where you are now. You took a job opportunity because it was easy and you could get money faster and could finally stop searching for a perfect job that might not exist. Another reason is that you have changed and your priorities or wants do not match the goals from the past that you are still holding onto. Have you ever heard someone say that they are in their current career field because they have dreamed about it since they were a child; yet they constantly complain or seem unhappy being at work?

Another real and common reason that people lose themselves is trying to make other people happy. It may sound selfless at the time, but doing something you genuinely do not want to do, just to please someone else, is one of the worst disservices you can do to yourself. Doing this can lead to resentment towards the person you wanted to help, unhappiness with yourself, and the eventual deterioration of your dreams. This is a typical occurrence for people in relationships. One person feels like they give too much, sacrifice what they want to make the other person happy, and constantly give up opportunities for the convenience of their significant other. That is when the phrase "I don't know who I am anymore, I need time to find myself" is brought up in conversation.

Your relationships, career, financial status, and success can all be saved if you are honest with who you are. Your purpose in life is not to make others happy, even if it means compromising your beliefs. It is time for you to reflect on who you are as a person. What do you value? What do you dislike doing? Do you still want the same things you wanted two, four, or ten years ago? How have you changed? Do you like who you are, or are you not a true representation of how you feel inside?

Chapter 3: Success Defined by Our Stages

Disregarding cultural traditions and customs, there is a huge difference in what progress and success looks like throughout our various stages of life. There is a common idea that as we become older, we become wiser but also less goal-oriented and less motivated. But the substitute for our lack of drive at an older age is the wide range of experiences that have supposedly taught us better than to fantasize about what could be or what might have been. This way of thinking may be what makes us worse at taking action and practicing leadership. Do you believe that as we age, the less we care about our work? If so, how does this mindset affect our initiative, leadership, happiness, and success?

In 2013, the Families and Work Institute concluded that people in the workforce started to lose their ambition to get promoted and look for chances to take on more responsibility near the age of thirty-five. Some researchers believe that the lack of ambition is correlated to the demands of starting a family. But there is more evidence that loss of motivation has more to do with our conditioned life patterns than a dissatisfaction with or distraction from our jobs. Studies have consistently shown that workers hit their peak in happiness at ages eighteen and eighty- two, and their lowest slope of unhappiness at the age of forty- six. This is when a mid- life crisis typically occurs.

The Economist defines this pattern the "U- bend" of life. When you are just starting out in life, you are excited about the possibilities and future responsibilities that are out there for you. The personification of this is the typical fresh- faced college grad who cannot wait to enter the job market and make his mark on the world. And how do his older and wiser coworkers respond? With smirks, headshakes, and the advice that one day he will understand that having a career is not what it is made out to be. But even with all the years of stress at the same company, older folks tend to be happier as they age: their sense of accomplishment, years of invaluable experience, and caring less about people pleasing. Not to mention they are no longer in the mist of their childrearing years.

It kind of sounds slightly depressing that most people are not happy unless they are really young and naïve, or old enough to know better. A study by Joan Broderick and Joseph Schwartz showed that the U- bend pattern reflects less stress in twenty- year olds as they progress through the workforce. This was then followed by a drastic increase in stress at the age of thirty, until mid-life, before falling once again. This mental pattern can have a serious impact on your progress and success, especially if you take it as your life's truth.

The fact of the matter is that we adopt similar behaviors as the people we are in closest proximity to. So, if your friends at work have negative mental attitudes and rationalize giving up on working towards exceling in the office, you most likely will as well. Regardless of your age, you have still required more knowledge in your years in the work force than you did during your time at school. Rather than simply using the minimum amount of effort and information to just get the job done, you should be using your unique perspective to enhance your work performance. You do not have to live up to the statistics that label you as the high- strung overworked middle- aged worker bee that these studies have made you out to be. Even if you are not at that point yet, know that you don't ever have to be that stereotype. Your age does not define your success or capability. You are never too old or too young to experience the best years of your life and live out your dreams.

Teresa Amabile and Steven Kramer found in their study "The Progress Principle" that employees will work harder and create new ideas when they are happier. This idea links to what we discussed in the first chapter; that when you interested and passionate enough to be happily engaged in your work, the more progress you will make and the more successful you will be. Sociological trends want us to believe that we are past our prime once we reach a certain age; that when we are younger and much older we experience the key years of promotion and success. But the reality is that there is no correlation between wisdom and leadership, age and leadership, nor wisdom and age.

So, while trends and studies may have you believe that you have wait for your opportune moment, or become settled with the fact that you have already missed it, there is really no stage in life that offers us the perfect chance to make it in the business world. While the things that make us happy change over time, your drive and yearning for happiness and success should not. Part of finding individual success is figuring out what your ambitions are at this stage in life. They may not be the same as they were when you were twenty years old, and that is okay. It natural, and even encouraged for you to let some dreams go if they do not make sense anymore in relation to your current place in life. Regardless of what stage in life you are in right now, you need to prioritize your goals and aspirations and take action towards them right now. Because *right now*, the present, is the perfect opportunity to work towards your goals. And that fact will never change.

Chapter 4: How to Refocus Your Mindset

Everyone wants to be successful in all areas of life. No one wants to be labeled as a failure or feel like they have not reached their peak potential. We all have this generic idea of success that does not specifically define any unique or individualistic goals for each person to achieve. If you think about it, success is practically impossible to achieve because we all think about it differently. Who are some people that you believe are successful? Some default answers may be: Bill Gates, Elon Musk, Brad Pitt and Angelina Jolie, Tony Robbins, Michael Jordan. While all of these people supposedly represent "success," they only have a few things in common: they have a decent amount of money, own businesses, and are celebrity figures. Is there much else that defines their success in life?

While many people correlate success with money, there is not much else that is constant with the general consensus of what defines success. Of course everyone wants to be happy, healthy, and have money to spend. But why do we not specify what success means to us as an individual? How do we really define success and apply *that* concept to our lives? Rather than taking a shot in the dark at an abstract idea. Because not everyone wants the same things. Not many people have the dream of being a celebrity or owning their own business. Even less people care about being in the spotlight and becoming a household name. Regardless of whether or not *you* want those things, creating your own definition of success will help you focus your mindset and create a focal point for your goals.

How Do We Define Success?

While money, fame, and power seem like a winning combination for the ideal image of success, establishing such high expectations can lead to disappointment and failure. Not to mention the unnecessary jealousy of those who do possess all of those things. Establishing this unrealistic definition of success for your life is what leads to mid- life crises and mental breakdowns. It also leads you to give up on any dreams you had and forget about what is really important to you. Too often, we create our definition of success off of what others believe it to be. But just like staying true to yourself, trying to mimic what someone else wants or is doing will only lead you to second guess yourself and go after goals that are not authentic to what you really want in life. This is completely unfair to you.

But just because money, fame, and power is not attainable for everyone, it does not mean that you should just give up on achieving success and living out your dreams. The definition of success is, the accomplishment or completion of a goal or purpose. Nowhere in the dictionary does it say "money and power." The United States is known for being a material- driven country—Americans believe that the more money and objects they have, the more they represent the image of success. But fancy cars, large houses, and designer clothes do not equate to fulfillment, happiness, or satisfaction. In other countries, success is defined by whether or not you can support your family, have an education, and live a long life. The point is that your definition of success should not compromise your priorities and values.

How do you create your own definition of success? By reevaluating your values, beliefs, and goals.

- Do You Believe Working Towards a Goal is Success?

- Are you taking action to make things happen?

- Are you accomplishing projects and tasks?

- Are you contributing to the world to make it a better place?

- Are you providing valuable insight or service?

- Do You Believe Happiness Equates to Success?

- Are you working at a job that makes you excited to get out of bed in the morning?

- Do you feel accomplished and happy after a full day's work?

- Do you feel more fulfilled and satisfied when you are happy?

- Do harmonious and fulfilling relationships make you feel happy?

- Do you feel like you have failed when you do not feel happy?

- Do You Believe Having a Balanced Life Means Success?

- Do you feel successful when you have balanced work with your personal life?

- Do you feel accomplished when you are able to give and equal amount of attention to multiple areas of your life?

- Do you feel accomplished when you have completed multiple tasks?

- Do you feel successful when you are doing well at work and your relationships are flourishing?

- Do You Define Success in Having a Fulfilling Relationship?

- Do you want a long- term fulfilling relationship?

- Is maintaining a happy relationship important to you?

- Do you feel fulfilled when you make your significant other happy?

- Do you feel fulfilled when you are surrounded by your loved ones?

Creating Your Own Definition of Success

Finding your own definition of success may be a little difficult, but once you establish it, you can work towards adjusting your mental state and achieving your dreams. Even the most stereotypical successful people in the world are still trying to figure out what is actually important to them. While the celebrities and political figures you see on television and in magazines might be rich, they are often surrounded with rumors of break- ups, divorce, feuds, and a whole slew of other problems. Do you really think these idolized celebrities truly feel successful when other areas of their life are falling apart?

The sooner you create your own definition of success, the easier it is to create goals that reflect true fulfillment—not just power or fame. Your definition of success and the proceeding goals should reflect what is most important to you. How do you know what you value the most? Picture yourself with all the money and time what you want. What would you do with it? Would you help others? Build your own in- house gym? Would you invest in developing your own business? Who would you want to share it with?

Answering these questions will help you create your own unique definition of success.

If you are still unsure of what is most important to you, turn to your mentors and other inspirations. How to your colleges and favorite authors define success? This subject has long been debated amongst philosophers and entrepreneurs for decades. Even if you just type your biggest inspiration into Google with the word "success," you will find plenty of articles about how that person views success and what is truly important. Sometimes, hearing what really rich or famous people value puts our values into perspective. If someone who has more money than you will ever make comments about ten other things that they think are more important, maybe they are on to something about how we view success in comparison to their life.

But your own definition of success does not have to be based off of your career. It can be defined by your relationships, health and fitness goals, and a dozen other small goals that can shape you into the best version of yourself. For many people, making money is just a stepping stone on the road to success, not the real definition of it. Money is just a tool that can be used to accomplish your primary goals in life. And once you have figured out what success means to you, you can define the rest of your goals to reflect it. But having goals does not mean creating a whole bucket list of things to do. Having two or three primary goals will help you stabilize your mental state and achieve everything you have ever dreamed of.

Redefining Failure

When you redefine how your view success, you are also redefining what failure means to you. While failing truly means giving up on achieving success, your focused and limited goals make failing a lot less scary and less likely to happen. The point of reading this book and setting new goals is to find enough motivation and passion in achieving your dreams that failing is simply not an option. That your enthusiasm and motivation is too strong to keep you from letting yourself fail, not matter how challenging it gets.

Whether you are an amateur entrepreneur or a professional trying to be more successful in your career, you have most likely experienced failure or a challenge that has hurt your self- esteem. If you have not had this experience yet, then you are going to. It is a normal part of life and the journey towards achieving your goals.

If failing means giving up and not achieving your dreams, then you can't call a roadblock a failure. Filing for bankruptcy after your first business venture fails is not a true failure if you refuse to give up on your goal of being an entrepreneur. Every day is a new chance to take action towards achieving your dreams and living up to your own definition of success.

Chapter 5: Setting New Goals and Finding Your Purpose

Excuses are the reason that you have lost motivation and ambition in the pursuit of achieving your goals. Really, we provide excuses for even the smallest of failed tasks. "I ordered Chinese food take- out because I was too tired to cook." "I had a long day at work, so I am going to skip the gym." These common, every day rationalizations are keeping you from living out your purpose and going after your goals. But where does your lack of motivation stem from? These are the most frequently used excuses that are used to convince yourself to put off your goals for "one more day:"

- Lack of confidence in your abilities

- Believing that there are other, more important things to do instead

- Fear of failure because of past experiences

- Fear of what other people might say or think about you

- Being too worried or stressed to get things done

- Acting out of the habit of procrastination

- Pure laziness

- A lack of stimuli or incentives to get yourself motivated

Acknowledging and understanding that you can change your mental state and attitude towards these rationalizations will help your overcome them. If you want to improve your life and become successful, you need to spark that flame of motivation and ambition. You need to condition your brain to work towards improving your life by telling yourself every day, multiple times each day, how much your success suffers by using these excuses.

If you need incentives for going after your dreams while still trying to accomplish normal, everyday tasks, then work towards building up a positive mental attitude. Otherwise, old habits of lethargy and laziness will settle back in. It is so easy to fall back into your routine of being passive towards your goals. But instead of playing the self-victimizing games and wallowing in pools of suffering, find enough motivation to take action and accomplish your goals! Just working towards your dreams will make enhance your mental state: helping you feel happier and satisfied.

Passivity and indifference is what kills motivation and weakens your drive for satisfaction. But if you are enthusiastic and actively working towards being happy, your motivation will become stronger and more forceful. You will be driven to act on your goals, distract your mind from difficulties, and focus on creating solutions and being successful. Fine out where you really need the motivation and do whatever you can to improve that area of your life. What are your real goals and what can you do every day to make them happen?

Here are some tips and strategies to strengthen your mindset and keep you motivated in reaching your goals:

- Do the dishes now, instead of later. (And "letting them soak" isn't a good excuse either.)

- Take the garbage out instead of rushing to do it in the morning or forgetting about it completely.

- Turn off the television and go for a walk.

- Clean the house and reorganize your dresser drawers.

- Pick a book and start reading it, even if you would rather be doing other things.

Keeping yourself busy and moving will also keep you motivated and enthusiastic. Lethargy sets in when you convince yourself to take a break and end up watching television for three hours. And while TV is a good distraction from stress, it also distracts you from doing what is important.

15 Positive Affirmations for Building a Strong Mental State

1. I know what I want, my goals are clearly defined. I will pursue them today with determination, enthusiasm, and belief that I can accomplish them.

2. Every obstacle that blocks my way, every challenge that I face is an opportunity to prove my strength and get closer to my goals.

3. When I feel stressed today, I will relax and gather my thoughts before moving forward with my next move.

4. Today, I will show love and thankfulness towards the people in my life who mean the most to me.

5. Today, I will set an example for my friends, coworkers, family, and children – because they will learn more when I lead by example, and actions speak louder than words.

6. I will go through life in the joy and reality of being alive and capable. My past does not affect me, my future is unknown, so I will be thankful and joyful for every moment I have.

7. I am the architect of my life. I choose how to build and shape it, according to my wants and needs. I have

33

already built its foundations, now I will choose its contents.

8. I forgive the people who have hurt and discouraged me in the past, and I willfully detach myself from them.

9. I know and believe that I possess all of the qualities needed to be successful. My business is growing and thriving every single day.

10. Happiness is a choice, and I choose to be happy. My happiness comes from my own accomplishments and all of the blessings I have in my life.

11. Even though I am going through difficult times, I know that they are only a short phase in my life. My ideal future is the projection of what I envision now – and that image drives me to keep working hard.

12. My time and efforts are supported by the universe, and I control whether or not my dreams come true. Therefore, my dreams will manifest into reality.

13. My challenges are moving out of my way, faster than I know. And I that my path is filled with greatness.

14. I will go out into the world with an open mind – free from fear of judgement or criticism from others and myself. I control how destiny.

15. I deserve real happiness. I am confident that I will fight for my happiness, because my drive is greater than the challenges I face.

Chapter 6: Keeping Your Inner- Child Alive

At this moment in time, you are every age that you have ever been throughout your life. Holistic doctors and therapists believe that this statement is true because a "perfect" childhood does not exist, and therefore, you probably did not get everything you needed at various ages. Because of this, your inner child may still by trying to satisfied those neglected needs without even consciously realizing it. The greatest problem that stems from this is that if you do not consciously work towards fulfilling those needs now, you will unintentionally sabotage what you want most in your adult life.

Everyone moves through live in their own unique way. The same goes for children. As a child, when your parents, peers, and teachers did not understand your unique natural way of living, they criticized you or tried to stop it. Although their judgements seemed precautionary at the time, their opinions became stories that you believed about yourself as you grew older. As an adult, you may still shame yourself for reasons you were criticized as a child. If you do not stop this behavior, then you will sabotage yourself from achieving your true potential.

What Criticisms Did You Hear as a Child?

Every child shows signs of one of four dominant forms of expressions. Therefore, every individual child frequently hears a specific pattern of criticism from others who do not understand their true nature. Take a look through the following limiting messages that you might have heard as a child. Then, take a moment to check in with yourself – do you still believe these judgements?

35

Child Type 1 – Fun- Loving and Carefree

Fun- loving children are extroverted, social, and bring a ton of positive hyper energy to everything they do. But in response, they are told to sit down, be quiet, and stay calm. Did you hear any of these things as a child?

- You are too silly.

- You talk too much.

- You are always changing your mind; make up your mind already.

- You move around too much – settle down and be quiet.

Child Type 2 – Sensitive and Shy

Children who are naturally emotionally connected with the rest of the world are sensitive. If you identify with this child type, you may have been told to talk louder and felt invisible or unnoticed a lot of the time. Did you hear any of these things as a child?

- You are too shy.

- Why are indecisive, hurry up and choose.

- You ask too many questions.

- You are too sensitive, stop reacting so negatively to everything.

-

Child Type 3 – Determined and Task- Oriented

Children who are go- getters tend to be dynamic and physical. However, many adults felt frustrated with you and tried to hold you back. Did you hear any of the following statements as a child?

- You tire me out.

- Stop being bossy and pushy.

- You are way too loud, settle down.

- Say excuse me and stop being demanding.

Child Type 4 – Serious and Curious

Serious—type children are knowledge- driven and view themselves and the authority figure of their own world. They do not like being put on the spot or judged based on who they are. If you believe that you were are serious child, you might have heard:

- You take everything too seriously—why don't you smile more?

- Stop being such a know- it- all.

- You are not outgoing or social enough.

- Don't be such a goody- two-shows for the rules.

Your inner child was told on a consistent basis to be the exact opposite of who they are. Every child, at every age, needs to know that they are loved unconditionally and able to have the love they deserve. If you feel like things are just not working out for you or that life is not going the way you wished it would, reflect on how loved you feel overall in your life. Do you believe you are deserving of love, just as you are? If not, then practice these powerful exercises to fit your inner child's needs. This is enable you to become a stronger and more balanced adult.

Exercise #1

This exercise is a basic method of establishing a connect with your inner child to promote healing. You want to keep your inner child alive and happy, because they are the most genuine, authentic, passionate version of yourself.

Find a comfortable place to sit or lay down. If you can, try to find a picture of yourself from when you were five years old or younger. This will help establish the emotional connection faster. Now, picture your inner child, yourself as a child during a vulnerable moment in your childhood. Tell your inner child that they are loved and that you are going to take care of them. Tell them that everything your parents, teachers, and peers told you were out of fear and misunderstanding. Tell your inner child that it is okay to be yourself, and the embrace all the things that make you unique.

Exercise #2

Every day, tell your inner child these sixth truths to promote healing. These statements are most likely the things that your inner child feels sabotaged of. Now, you must take on the role and the nurturer and love yourself.

1. I Love You

Needing to hear you tell yourself that you love who you are does not mean that your parents and family did not or does not love you. As a child, you may have believed that you needed to accomplish goals to be lovable. That our parents' and friends' love was based on whether or not you got good grades, made the sport's team, or lived up to their expectations. You may not have had parents who reminded you that you deserved to be loved, regardless of how much you accomplished. In fact, many children grow up in families that view showing love and sensitivity as signs of weakness.

But you can show yourself love now. You can tell yourself that you are loveable and deserve love in your life. Whenever you see your reflection in a mirror, tell yourself "I love you." Do in times of trouble and strife. Love yourself unconditionally.

2. I Hear You and I am Listening

For many of us, when we feel hurt or misunderstood, we push our feelings down and try to stay strong. This reaction to pain and sadness is a reflection of what we were told as children, "If you don't stop crying, I'll give you something to cry about." "Wipe that frown off your face or I'll do it for you." But those feelings of unhappiness and discontent do not just disappear; they stay inside of us, affecting our choices as adults.

These feelings will continue to fester inside of us until we make a conscious effort to hear them. Pushing your feelings down will affect your relationships and keep you from sticking up for yourself. Instead of repressing the voice of your inner child, tell them "I hear you and I am going to help you work through it. Everything will be okay."

3. You Did Not Deserve This

As children, most us of believed that we deserved to be punished, shamed, or abandoned. We believed that we were bad and did something wrong, so we should be held accountable for our actions. But this is not true. In most cases, the people who punished or hurt us did not know any other way to cope. Maybe your parents were physically abused as children, so that is the only way they know how to parent their children. But children are innocent and pure of intention. They do not deserve to be abused or abandoned. It is not their fault because they did not have the mental capacity to understand this.

4. I Forgive You

One of the fastest methods of emotional destruction is allowing yourself to hold onto regret and shame. We do things as children that lead us to be punished or experience consequences that we felt we did not deserve. But now that you know you did not deserve to suffer and take the blame, you can finally forgive yourself for not doing something that could have been done better. As children and adult, we are only human; and humans are imperfect beings. It is okay to have messed up, and it is time to forgive yourself and let it go.

5. Thank You

Your inner child has never given up on you and has been with you through every challenge in life. It is time to thank your inner child for being there with you and supporting you with strength and perseverance. Thank your inner child for always trying to protect you, even though it may have been by holding on to painful memories. Your inner child deserves respect, not criticism; so thank them for always being there.

6. You Did the Best You Could

Children feel the constant pressure to be the best, to overachieve, and to meet someone else's expectations. The need to be perfect causes a great amount of emotional and mental strain. These expectations are first imbedded by parents, but we adopt them for ourselves as we grow older. We are constantly demanding ourselves to be better, but always end up feeling like we are not good enough. Remind your inner child that you did the best you could and are still doing the best you can. You deserve that recognition. Once we let go of our need to be perfect, the fear of failing fades. We can allow ourselves to embrace change and watch new and unfamiliar circumstances unfold.

When you are a little kid, working harder at becoming better at something is much easier. Do you remember excitedly getting home from school, throwing your backpack on the floor, and diving into your passion? Maybe it was riding your bike, playing catch, beating a new video game, or practicing gymnastics? You knew that if you wanted to get better at something, you had to practice every day and spend time working on it. You kept your focus and drive the whole time, even when you were supposed to be paying attention to something else.

Of course there were times of frustration and disappointment, but you never gave up on yourself. You knew that if you really wanted to get the outcome you wanted, and believed it was possible, then you kept working at it. So what happens to this mindset when we become adults? How did we lose the understanding of mastering a skill or goal? Many people believe that we lose this mindset because we do not have time in our adult lives to spend on our passion. But true passion and motivation overtakes your life; making sleeping and eating seem strenuous because it is time wasted.

Other people blame their lack of ambition on a complete lack of passion. We numb ourselves to the ability of feeling excitement and curiosity, which leads us to take action in the first place. But this is not a lack of passion, but a symptom of forgetting the joy that working on your passion brings you. We are too afraid of feeling uncomfortable or vulnerable to pain and failure that we sabotage our own success.

Do not be afraid to be a beginner at something new, regardless of your age or where you are in life. When we are children, we base off our abilities to succeed off of our peer's. If Jill can ride a bike, then why shouldn't I? You use other people's success as motivation to succeed as well. This enabled you to keep practicing until you accomplished your goals. However, as adults we only look at how our peers are different from us; they are smarter, richer, or luckier, therefore they were able to succeed. You would rather believe that there is something wrong with you than take a risk to potentially fail.

Success can only be achieved when you devote time and effort towards attaining your ideal outcome. Never stop trying to achieve your dreams. They are worth the effort and struggle. Turn your gaze inward and reflect on what you want most in life. Give your inner child the pleasure and satisfaction that they have been starved of for so long. Give yourself permission to start living your dreams.

Conclusion

Thank you again for downloading *Success: A Handbook for Developing the Right Mindset and Achieving Your Dreams*!

I hope this book was able to help you to alter your mindset and motivate you to achieve your dreams and go after your goals. For many of us, it is our own mental roadblocks that inhibit us from taking charge and attacking our goals.

The next step is to use everything that you have learned in this book to overcome your mental barriers and live the life of your dreams.

Finally, if you enjoyed this book, please take the time to share your thoughts and post a review on Amazon. It'd be greatly appreciated!

Thank you and good luck!

About the Author

Fred Mercado is the president of Mercado Consulting; A Consulting company with a focus in the Enterprise and Wireless industry in North America and the Caribbean and Latin America - CALA. He holds an AS Degree in Avionics from Embry-Riddle Aeronautical University, a Bachelor of Science Degree in Business from Excelsior College of New York, and MBA in International Business from American Intercontinental University of Chicago.

Fred is an experienced business executive with over 30 years of professionalism in the business and telecommunication industry. He is a well-known leader and achiever as his expertise expands through domestic and international markets. He has worked in various executive level positions with several well established organizations including his time with Wireless Facilities Inc., Crown-Castle International, MetroPCS, and at McCaw Cellular Communications/AT&T Wireless. Fred also serves as a Board Advisor and technical & business consultant to several companies in the telecommunications industry.

Fred also has several internationally recognized certificates including Project Management Professional (PMP), Corporate Governance (Sarbanes Oxley - SOX) from Tulane University, Negotiations, and Organisational Behaviour, from Heriot-Watt University in the UK and is a certified Total Quality Management (TQM) Instructor. He has written several industrial papers that gained the attention of many and as an author writing a series of books to share his experience, knowledge and expertise in a bid to further educate, assist and build new leaders. His series covers every aspect in establishing knowledge and expertise in the field of Business, Project Management, and overall Leadership.

You can learn more about Fred by visiting:

www.mercadoconsulting.com

www.fredmercado.com

https://www.linkedin.com/in/fredmercado

Also visit my website at www.thenewleaders.com to join the team of leaders making a difference in today's society.

Bonus:

Subscribe to The New Leaders and receive a free eBook on Leadership.

Visit my site at http://www.thenewleaders.com and join my email list. When you sign up I will send you updates on advancements, news, educational information, and opportunities to help advance your leadership ambitions and skills.

I also have a Free eBook that I will send you upon joining the list. The ebook is full of relevant and extremely useful information on becoming a great leader, and a great source of information to home the leadership skills you already have.

It is free with no strings attached, just my way of thanking you for purchasing my book and joining the league of today influential leaders.

www.ingramcontent.com/pod-product-compliance
Lightning Source LLC
Chambersburg PA
CBHW070227210526
45169CB00023B/1196